Christine
Follow your
dreams!
♡ Diane

THE
Mastermind
EFFECT

W0013818

The *Mastermind* Effect

Amplify Your Success Together

DIANE CUNNINGHAM ELLIS

© 2023 Diane Cunningham Ellis

ISBN: 978-1-7346066-4-5

All rights reserved. No part of this publication may be reproduced, distributed, or transmitted in any form or by any means, including photocopying, recording or other electronic or mechanical methods, without prior written permission of the publisher, except in the case of brief quotations embodied in critical views and certain other noncommercial uses permitted by copyright law. For permission requests, write to the publisher, addressed "Attention: Permissions Request," at the email address below.

Diane@DianeCunningham.com

www.DianeCunningham.com

Printed in the United States of America.

I dedicate this book to the women and men that I have walked alongside in my own mastermind and in the masterminds that I am part of. Thank you for teaching me, loving me, showing me the way, and helping me to see my own magnificence.

God, thank you for the gift of community and for teaching us the power of a group through the 12 disciples that you gathered up for Jesus.

"For where two or three are gathered in my name, I am there…"

MATTHEW 18:20

Contents

Acknowledgments

Thank you to the women I have coached, mentored and taught over the past 25 years, in groups, workshops, a membership, retreats, and now masterminds. I am honored to bravely walk by your side!

Thank you to Callie Revell who helps me behind the scenes with every book, website page, image, document, and Zapier link and makes me look so very good.

To my amazing husband, Jim, who has been along for the ride and supported my "crazy ideas" since our very first date in 2015. Thank you for "trudging this road of happy destiny" with me in marriage and entrepreneurship. I am so proud of you and of US!

To Mary and Michelle, my business bestie team that bonded forever after our car accident in May 2023 . . . Let the adventures continue (without us getting hit by a semi-truck next time)!

And to God, the creator of my passion, dreams, and this book, may I always honor you with my work and allow it to be a vessel that serves the world!

Foreword

CODY BURCH

A Mastermind saved my business (and maybe my life). It sounds weird, but it's true. In June 2022, I shut down my six-year-old Digital Agency to take a full-time job with my favorite coaching client.

The dream job turned out to be a nightmare and I was abruptly fired six months later.

I was shocked. I was depressed. I was lost.

A few days after being terminated, I scanned through my emails and folders to see what I was still a part of. I remembered I was a member of a business Mastermind that hosted monthly Q&A sessions and hotseats.

Even though I had been in the Mastermind for four years, I had never attended one of the calls. I jumped on the call and sheepishly put my hand up when it was time to share. I tearfully admitted I had just been fired and didn't know what to do next.

The love, care, and support from the Mastermind in that moment was tangible. It was like they reached through the computer screen and gave me a big ol' hug.

Within a few weeks of that call, I was back on my feet making offers and getting clients. I jumped on the next monthly call (two in a row!) and shared the momentum and success. I haven't missed a call or meet-up since then. And you know what? I love Masterminds so much I started one of my own.

Just five months after getting let go, I hosted an in-person experience. Twelve showed. Nine joined my Mastermind. Now, I'm a member of three different Masterminds around specific topics and I can't imagine doing business any other way. The concepts Diane shares in this book are sound, simple, and effective.

I met Diane at a Mastermind. She joined my Mastermind. If you're thinking of joining a Mastermind, or starting your own, there is no one more thoughtful, warm, and friendly than Diane. You're in good hands.

Enjoy the book.

Introduction

I t was 2014. I was watching my bank account dwindle down to nothing. It was a cold Texas week in November, and money was leaving fast and not enough payments on the horizon. I was panicked. I was frantic. At the time, I had 4 self-published books, was leading the National Association of Christian Women Entrepreneurs (NACWE) (which I had founded in 2010), and yet didn't have enough money for my upcoming payments for my house and my car as a single entrepreneurial woman.

I felt like a fraud to all of my clients. Imposter syndrome all around. This was in spite of my Masters Degree in Education, a plethora of certifications, and years in business.

And then my coach had the foresight to suggest I create a one-year mastermind . . . and everything changed.

I started my first year-long mastermind in January 2015 and haven't looked back. I am now a master-mind coach and trusted advisor to those who want to create their own mastermind, or you can start by joining mine (if you are the right fit).

Now, let's go farther back in the story. I first heard about masterminds in 2008-2009 or so and took a certification from the Rescue Institute to become a Mastermind Executive Coach. Then, I offered my first 90-day mastermind type of program for women in 2009. I called it Go B.I.G. Success Sisters (Beyond Imaginable Goals).

Then I stopped for a while as I was busy as the Founder and President of NACWE from 2010 on as we were offering live conferences, webinars, virtual summits, and coaching events. But in 2015, I took a suggestion from my coach and created my first long-term mastermind, Brave Adventures Inner Circle, and it was $12,000. Two women joined for a year together. It was life-changing for me and for them.

What attracted me to the mastermind concept is that it combined coaching, community, collaboration, and creativity. It honestly seemed too good to be true. Too fun. Too easy.

And it saved my business.

In fact, it changed the trajectory of my life, which is what I will be sharing in this book.

So, back to that holiday season of 2014 . . .

I quickly pulled together a sales page, decided on a name, and offered it to a few women. To my complete shock, two women paid in full at $12,000 for a year. It transformed my life in a myriad of ways as I look back on that moment in time. We went on trips, and we met quarterly at my home for two-day events. We had group calls, and they each got access to private coaching.

Since 2015, I have hosted 6-12 month masterminds for Christian women entrepreneurs, serving dozens of women. We have had up to 16 at one time, and we have now been in various forms for almost ten years. My mastermind is not industry specific, but it is only for Christian women entrepreneurs. All types of women business owners are enrolled, but I attract many coaches and counselors, authors, and speakers.

I have also done mini-masterminds using the power of a tool called Voxer. This allows for an asynchronous experience of a mastermind inside of the app. Sometimes, I have added Zoom calls as a BONUS. These have been for 2-4 weeks to provide a short sample of the life-changing power of a mastermind (again, The Mastermind Effect).

I have also hosted mastermind days and retreats—and helped my clients create their own mastermind offers.

Each year or season, I have assessed what has been working and what needs to change. I survey the group. I get on calls with the members to discuss ideas and options. I consider what is important to keep and what needs to stop, adapt, or be archived.

We have done Mindset Calls and offered optional 12-Step type of Recovery Calls. We have done 2-3 live events a year. We have gone on trips and adventures to Colorado, weekends in North Carolina, and hosted virtual summits.

This book is for you if:

- You want to join a mastermind or create your own

- You want the inside details of the power of higher-level conversations

- You desire ongoing community and ideas that will transform your business acumen

This book is NOT for you if:

- You want to only do workshops, courses, and sprint events (challenges, mini-courses)

- You want to stay in the one-on-one mindset for your coaching

- You are afraid of commitment

Over these years of learning, I have discovered the five key elements for mastermind success and will be sharing in detail about them in forthcoming chapters.

► Community

► Collaboration

► Communication

► Consistency

► Commitment

This is what I have now deemed, THE MASTER-MIND EFFECT. All of this leads to being immersed in high-level deep conversations, skilled group dynamics, time management, leadership, give and take, commitment, ownership, trust, learning, and emotional connection.

In my journey, I have developed a multifaceted approach. We have met weekly, bi-monthly, using Zoom, Facebook groups, live events, and recently the addition of a Voxer or Telegram channel.

I now use an application process. I didn't start that until a few years ago. My mastermind groups have always been paid, and the price has varied many times over the years.

It's important to have time for everyone to share at various points of the group meetings with wins, invite people to have hotseat times, lead group discussions on teaching topics that we bring to the table, provide prompts, encourage off-topic discussions in-between meetings, and embrace humor and humility.

The diversity of the group is what helps it stay vibrant and interesting. Different types of businesses, professional experience, ages, life stories. And even different levels of monetary success.

Guest Experts have been a key part of the mastermind as they share on their expert topic and provide value to the group.

WHAT IS THE MASTERMIND EFFECT?

Think of it as the secret sauce that amplifies individual brilliance into collective genius. It's the alchemy that happens when diverse minds converge in a space of trust, commitment, and openness. Each member comes in with their own unique set of skills and insights, but what they walk away with is exponentially greater: a synergistic blend of shared wisdom, support, and a powerhouse of actionable strategies.

In simple terms, the Mastermind Effect is the multiplier of your success, turning the impossible into the achievable.

There have been a few times that a member didn't click with another member and discussed it privately with me. Not everyone will become the best of friends in a mastermind cohort, and yet each person has value in the group. I have found that often a group "conflict" is a mirror to us of what we might need to learn for the bigger picture of our life journey. I believe that everything is a lesson.

I have had members drop out when it was not the right fit or a financial hardship was happening. And I once had to remove a member due to some personal challenges that were impacting her participation and the group as a whole. It is the mastermind facilitator's responsibility to keep the group a safe and sacred space for the bigger community.

In each chapter of the book, you will get glimpses of true stories from women in my Braver Together Mastermind and from the colleagues (men and women) that I know from my commitment in mastermind groups.

Using the power of a mastermind has saved my business and changed my life.

They have allowed me to use my greatest gifts as an expert, trusted advisor, former counselor, coach, consultant, and business woman.

What I love about hosting a mastermind:

I love to watch the women connect, create, and collaborate together. I love to shower them with gifts and referrals and opportunities. I love being able to get them the higher level deep curated community that they desire. I get to be a conduit.

Over the years, we have had groups that had a beginning and an end, but now my group runs ongoing.

Masterminds line up perfectly with my life mission statement:

My mission in life is to inspire women to dream big, catch on fire and change the world.

I wrote it in 2009. It was prompted by a quote from John Wesley:

"Catch on fire with enthusiasm and people will come from miles to watch you burn."

Here is a glimpse of what we are going to cover:

In Chapter 1, we will share The Magic of Masterminds.

- *This chapter explains the overview of a mastermind, myths, common things included and more.*

In Chapter 2 , we will dive deep into Community.

- *Community is where it all starts. It is the community that is created by the group, for the group to form genuine relationships. We will share tips on how to make your community feel connected and dynamic through the years.*

When we get to Chapter 3, it's all about Collaborations.

- *Collaborations are a key part of masterminding. Bouncing ideas off of each other, brainstorming together, and getting valuable instant feedback will bring about business breakthroughs faster than you can imagine.*

Chapter 4 takes us into the keystone of Communication.

- *Clarity of communication for the facilitator and the members is crucial. We will share about unique ways to facilitate honest discussions and why listening is just as vital as speaking your truth.*

And then we go to the wealth of Chapter 5: Consistency.

- *Unpacking why consistency is the "C" that many overlook, yet it's essential for long-term success. I will share stories from lessons learned in 9 years of masterminds and mistakes made along the way.*

In Chapter 6, we unpack a fear-provoking word, Commitment.

- *In order to have a successful mastermind, members need to be committed to the process. Everything from showing up on time to contributing your unique skills. The committed group is life changing and business expanding.*

We conclude with a chapter on how to cultivate your own mastermind mindset for ongoing success and then a bonus chapter about the gift of curiosity in your pursuit of clarity. Curiosity is a gift.

Finally, I will provide you with a treasure chest of gifts in the Resources section that is updated and current on my website and along the way in the links!

Ready to grab my FREE Mastermind Checklist? Go here now:

www.MastermindChecklist.com

Mastermind Moments are included to share insights from women in my mastermind and people I know from the masterminds that I participate in!

Don't worry. This will be a fun journey in a short book!

Let's dive in!

The *Mastermind* Effect

COMMUNITY

The reason masterminds are effective is the community component for ongoing growth, learning and expansion.

COLLABORATION

Collaborations multiply in a mastermind by nature of the sharing of ideas, resources, experiences and opportunities.

COMMUNICATION

Communication lays a foundation of higher level conversations, about mindset, messaging, marketing and more.

CONSISTENCY

By being together on an ongoing basis, we know each other deeply and remind each other of our strengths, gifts, talents and abilities.

COMMITMENT

With the commitment of a mastermind, you have the gift of transformation and the trust of knowing WE are all here together.

CHAPTER ONE

The Magic of Masterminds

Call it a clan, call it a network, call it a tribe, call it a family. Whatever you call it, whoever you are, you need one.

JANE HOWARD

Welcome to the inner sanctum of masterminds, a realm that I've navigated for nearly a decade. If you're seeking an introductory fluff piece on the power of communal learning, Be assured, this isn't it. Instead, I invite you to embark on a transformative journey—one that can alter your professional landscape and personal development in ways you've yet to imagine.

Defining the Mastermind

Firstly, let's articulate what a Mastermind truly is: it's an elite alliance of professionals intensely committed to mutual growth and success. While the word "Mastermind" has often been diluted in the business vernacular, understand that genuine masterminds are more than mere meet-ups or networking opportunities. They are focused, collaborative efforts to tackle challenges, strategize solutions, and bring about real-world results.

Networking vs. Masterminding: Know the Difference

If you're under the impression that a mastermind is a glorified networking group, permit me to enlighten you. Networking often occurs on a surface level—you exchange business cards, perhaps engage in a little small talk, and move on. In a mastermind, you don't just exchange pleasantries; you exchange life-altering advice, strategies, and insights. The relationships you cultivate here often become cornerstones for both personal and business growth.

The Catalog of Benefits

For the skeptics among you, allow me to catalog the undeniable benefits that come with participating in a bona fide mastermind. We're talking about accountability at its finest; a diversified portfolio of ideas; amplified problem-solving capacities; emotional sustenance; and perhaps most importantly, a circle of influence that compounds in value over time.

The Results Speak for Themselves

In my nine years of hosting masterminds, I've witnessed start-ups evolve into enterprises, freelancers rise to agency owners, and most importantly, individuals transform into better versions of themselves. The value derived from these group experiences is immeasurable and profoundly impacts all facets of life.

Every mastermind is different, but I have gathered up a list for you here based on what I have learned and experienced with my group and others.

As you can see, the options are endless. Just like entrepreneurship. If you are creating your own mastermind, be sure to make it your style.

I am a member of three masterminds right now:

#1 has 12 people and includes one live retreat each year and has another cohort that meets for people

THINGS THAT ARE COMMONLY INCLUDED IN MASTERMIND GROUPS

1. **Collaborative Learning:** Members bring diverse expertise, experiences, and insights, creating a rich environment for learning from each other.

2. **Accountability**: Group members hold each other accountable for setting and achieving their goals, ensuring consistent progress.

3. **Brainstorming Sessions:** Regular sessions where members come together to brainstorm ideas, solve challenges, and generate innovative solutions.

4. **Goal Setting:** Members set individual and group goals, providing a clear sense of purpose and direction.

5. **Structured Meetings:** Meetings follow a defined structure, allowing for focused discussions and efficient use of time.

6. **Feedback and Advice:** Members provide constructive feedback and offer valuable advice based on their unique perspectives.

7. **Networking Opportunities:** Masterminds create a platform for networking and building meaningful connections with like-minded individuals.

8. **Personal Development:** The collaborative environment encourages personal growth, self-awareness, and skill development.

9. **Resource Sharing:** Members share resources, tools, and recommendations to help each other overcome challenges and achieve their goals.

10. **Mutual Support:** The group provides emotional support during setbacks and celebrates each others' successes.

11. **Skill Exchange:** Members can exchange skills and knowledge, enhancing their abilities through peer-to-peer learning.

12. **Guest Experts:** Inviting guest experts to share their insights and expertise on specific topics relevant to the group's goals.

13. **Mastermind Hot Seats:** A member presents a challenge or opportunity, and the group provides focused feedback and suggestions.

14. **Problem Solving:** The collective intelligence of the group helps members solve complex problems more effectively.

15. **Motivation and Inspiration:** Being surrounded by motivated individuals inspires members to push their boundaries and strive for excellence.

16. **Confidence Building:** Positive reinforcement and encouragement from peers help build confidence in pursuing ambitious goals.

17. **Access to Different Perspectives:** Gain fresh perspectives from individuals with diverse backgrounds, industries, and viewpoints.

18. **Accountability Partners:** Members can form smaller subgroups or pairs to provide more focused accountability and support.

19. **Live Events:** Group members often gather two or three times a year for in-person retreats, adventures, guest experts and hotseats.

20. **Long-Term Relationships:** Mastermind groups often lead to lasting friendships and professional relationships.

21. **Continuous Learning:** Ongoing exposure to new ideas, strategies, and approaches keeps members on the cutting edge of their fields.

22. **Time Management:** The structured nature of mastermind meetings helps members manage their time more effectively.

23. **Supportive Environment:** A safe and non-judgmental space for sharing challenges, setbacks, and triumphs.

24. **Group Dynamics Expertise:** Learn about group dynamics, communication, and leadership skills through hands-on experience.

25. **Personal Satisfaction:** Contributing to others' success and growth is fulfilling and personally rewarding.

Remember that the specific elements and benefits of a mastermind group can vary based on the group's focus, goals, and the preferences of its members. Each group has a unique vibe.

You can get this list here and a few other resources at: www.MastermindChecklist.com

SCAN ME

on the other side of the world, based on time zones. This is a one-year commitment.

#2 has nine people and it was launched from an in-person three-day workshop. This is a six-month program and includes other live events, private Voxer coaching, trainings, and more.

#3 has 50 people, and we have four focused modules for the year and the curriculum is based on those trainings.

I love each of them for different reasons. I get access to people that I never would have met and learn things that I never would have imagined. My concepts of business have transformed based on the acumen of the people in the group and the synergy of the conversations that happen on Zoom, in Telegram/Voxer channels, and the wealth of knowledge shared. Again, I call this the Mastermind Effect.

Now, let's get rid of a few myths about masterminds, shall we?

You see, I had many myths about them for years, in spite of even already hosting my own. Can you even believe that? We can easily get caught up in our own old stories. As a former counselor, I admit that I do this, too. The scarcity thinking. Making decisions out of fear. Not feeling like we can "afford" something.

Fast forward to now. I am currently in two high-level masterminds, and throughout the book, I will be sharing many stories from my own masterminds and the ones that I am a member of to give you some tangible examples. I cannot imagine not being in a mastermind at this stage of my business, and I hope you feel the same way after reading this book. The value is priceless.

Mastermind Myths

Mastermind groups are often touted as the secret sauce to personal and professional success, offering a space for people to share resources, knowledge, and support. However, like any tool or resource, mastermind groups aren't without their limitations or misconceptions.

Here are some common myths surrounding mastermind groups:

Myth 1: Instant Success

Reality: Many people think that just by joining a mastermind group, they're guaranteed to see instant success in their endeavors. While it's true that you can gain valuable insights, you still have to put in the work. Mastermind groups offer support and advice, but they aren't a shortcut to success.

Myth 2: Group Wisdom is Always Right

Reality: While a collective group often has diverse skills and experiences, it's not a guarantee that the group's advice is always correct. Groupthink can sometimes lead to decisions that aren't actually in your best interest. It's essential to think critically and consult other sources.

Myth 3: Expensive Groups are Better

Reality: Some people assume that the more expensive a mastermind group is, the better the quality or results. While higher costs can filter for more serious participants, it doesn't necessarily correlate with better outcomes. Many affordable or even free mastermind groups can offer immense value.

Myth 4: Everyone is Equally Committed

Reality: Not all members in a mastermind group will have the same level of commitment or engagement. Some may be there just for networking, some may not contribute much, and others might dominate conversations. Group dynamics can make or break the effectiveness of a mastermind group.

Myth 5: Mastermind Groups Replace Professional Services

Reality: Mastermind groups should not replace professional services like legal advice, financial planning, or medical consultation. While peer advice can be valuable, it isn't a substitute for specialized expertise.

Myth 6: All Mastermind Groups Are Structured the Same Way

Reality: Mastermind groups can be highly variable in how they are structured, in terms of meeting frequency, membership, focus, and governance. Assuming that what works in one group will work in another can be a mistake.

Myth 7: You Only Need to Take, Not Give

Reality: One of the fundamental values of a mastermind group is reciprocity. People who come only to take from the group and not give back in terms of support, resources, or time will likely find that the group is less beneficial for them as well.

Myth 8: Virtual Groups are Less Effective

Reality: In-person interaction can be beneficial, but virtual mastermind groups can also be highly effective. They offer more flexibility and can bring in a diverse set of people who might not otherwise be able to participate.

Myth 9: Bigger Groups Offer More Value

Reality: While a larger group may provide a wider range of perspectives, it can also make it difficult for each member to get personalized attention and value. Sometimes smaller, more focused groups can offer more targeted benefits.

Understanding these myths can help you make an informed decision about joining a mastermind group and how to make the most of it if you do. Or how to know what you desire to create your own! Want my help? Just set up a call.

I created a FREE Resource that includes this list and others for you:

www.DianeCunningham.com/BookResources

In summary, the true magic of a mastermind lies not in its structure, but in its dynamic capability to serve as a catalyst for transformation. As you navigate the subsequent chapters, I challenge you to disengage from any preconceived notions you have about collaborative success.

Brace yourself for an enlightening journey that distills my years of expertise into actionable insights. And if you are ready to start getting my help in creating your own mastermind, I would love to support you on this journey with a private Create Your Mastermind VIP Day. Or we would love to welcome you into the Braver Together Mastermind family.

QUESTIONS TO ASK BEFORE JOINING A MASTERMIND

FORMAT

☐ How long is the commitment? A year? 6 months?
☐ What is included? Weekly coaching? Bi-weekly groups? Live events? Facebook Group? Voxer or Telegram Channel?
☐ Is there a way to get private support from the facilitator, if desired?
☐ Are there any bonuses?
☐ Is there access to any courses?
☐ Is there a monthly or quarterly focus?

VIBE

☐ What types of people are enrolled?
☐ What is the feeling of the group?
☐ Does the group have an underlying theme?
☐ Is it specific to a certain type of member or diverse?
☐ What real life results have members gotten from being a part?

CONTENT

☐ What courses are included, if any?
☐ Do you get access to anything else the coach/leader offers during your time enrolled?
☐ Is there a success path for members to get the most value?
☐ Do you get an onboarding call?
☐ Do you get feedback from the group on your own content or bonus coaching from a copywriting coach?
☐ Does the coach/facilitator invite members to collaborate on content creation?

RESULTS

☐ Are there testimonials from those enrolled?
☐ Do you know anyone that is a part of the group who you can ask questions before making the commitment?
☐ Do you want to learn from the people and be a valuable member who is committed and willing to connect?
☐ What is your goal for joining this group?
☐ How will you know that the investment is worth it?

Mastermind Moment

from Diana Journy

Transforming My Coaching Practice: The Power of the Braver Together Mastermind
A Catalyst for Change

Before joining the Braver Together Mastermind, my coaching primarily focused on aiding women recovering from betrayal and assisting couples through the labyrinth of infidelity. This group encouraged me to think creatively and broaden my approach. I explored a range of new delivery methods, from virtual 1-on-1 sessions via Zoom to breaking intensive three-day couple retreats into more manageable segments.

Navigating New Horizons

The mastermind experience exposed a need for expanding my coaching demographic. I realized that my skills could serve not just women healing from betrayal, but also those entering new phases of life or those seeking a stronger voice in their relationships. Diane's guidance helped me take the significant step of establishing a new, focused website for my women-centric coaching. Alongside our couples' platform, "The Journey Through," this new website is about me, as a coach and allows me to reach a broader spectrum of clients.

The Community Advantage

What sets the Braver Together Mastermind apart is its community element. The group functions as an invaluable network of entrepreneurial women, providing a rich soil where novel ideas can grow. This communal support is the epitome of a modern business think-tank, complete with a diverse set of perspectives and entrepreneurial experiences.

The Diane Effect

When Diane shares her wisdom, it's not a mere exchange of information; it's an investment in each member's growth. Whether it's revealing the intricacies of effective Facebook posting or demonstrating the value of outsourcing certain skills, her insights have been transformative for my business.

A Paradigm Shift

Joining this mastermind group shifted not just my business model but also my mindset. I've begun exploring new avenues that allow for a more balanced life, enabling me to dedicate time to the essential people in my life, such as my grandchildren. In summary, the Braver Together Mastermind has been an invaluable asset, not just for my business growth but also for my personal development. I owe a great deal of this success to Diane's expert coaching.

www.DianaJourny.com

Questions to Ponder

If you are considering JOINING A MASTERMIND:

- What interests you about joining a mastermind?

- Why do you believe it could transform your business?

- What myths do you need to let go of related to masterminds?

If you are considering CREATING A MASTERMIND:

- Why do you want to offer a mastermind?

- What clients do you already have who might be a good fit?

- What dreams do you have for how a mastermind could transform your business?

YOU WON'T KNOW UNTIL YOU GO.

IT'S WORTH IT.

Let's explore!

The *Mastermind* Effect

COMMUNITY

The reason masterminds are effective is the community component for ongoing growth, learning and expansion.

COLLABORATION

Collaborations multiply in a mastermind by nature of the sharing of ideas, resources, experiences and opportunities.

COMMUNICATION

Communication lays a foundation of higher level conversations, about mindset, messaging, marketing and more.

CONSISTENCY

By being together on an ongoing basis, we know each other deeply and remind each other of our strengths, gifts, talents and abilities.

COMMITMENT

With the commitment of a mastermind, you have the gift of transformation and the trust of knowing WE are all here together.

CHAPTER TWO

Cultivate Your Community

> The greatness of a community is most accurately
> measured by the compassionate actions
> of its members.
>
> CORETTA SCOTT KING

I f Chapter 1 served as your introduction to the profound concept of Masterminds, consider this chapter the unveiling of its backbone—Community. You see, no matter how brilliant or driven an individual might be, they operate within the context of a wider social fabric. The essence of a mastermind is undeniably shaped by its members, by the community that surrounds it.

What is a community?

Community: a group of people living in the same place or having a particular characteristic in common. This could be geographical, like a neighborhood, or based on shared interests, beliefs, or goals.

Community: The Heart of the Matter

The notion that "it takes a village" resonates profoundly within mastermind groups. Community is the social glue that bonds members one-to-one, providing a robust network of support and accountability. The synergy generated through diverse skills and perspectives enriches the group's knowledge pool, leading to better decision-making and problem-solving. In essence, a strong community within a mastermind elevates the individual accomplishments to collective triumphs.

One of the members of my Braver Together Mastermind, Allison McNeil, said this: "If 'two heads are better than one,' then a community makes an ensemble of great ideas, encouragement, inspiration, 'spark,' and connection. Allison McNeil is a former teacher and now a Mental Health Counselor who happily joined our group to expand her business mindset and offer more value to her counseling and coaching clients. She found that the power of the group was life-changing to support her in new skills for entrepreneurship and things she did not learn in graduate school.

The Indispensable Element

Community isn't merely an optional add-on; it's an indispensable element. In the world of masterminds, a strong community serves as the conduit for transformative change, a framework that supports individual achievements while propagating collective wins. Your community sets the tempo, establishes the standards, and perpetuates the values that define your experience.

Strength in Diversity

In the microcosm of a mastermind, each member brings a unique blend of experiences, skills, and viewpoints. This diversity isn't just beneficial—it's vital. A homogeneous group is an echo chamber; a diversified group is a catalyst for innovation.

In my Braver Together Mastermind, we have a huge diversity of businesses:

Noelle owns two thriving childcare centers and has a membership for childcare center owners to help them succeed in a challenging market. She also now has a subscription box that she started during COVID using the power of playdough.

Susan is an author, coach, and former Registered Dietitian and former classroom teacher who now has a membership called Our World of Food Community where she offers training, food meet-ups, lessons, and more.

Cindy and her husband own a wood-fired pizza business called Consuming Fire where they serve pizza at events, weddings, farmers markets, and at monthly pizza parties in Wisconsin. She also has her own wellness business to transform women's lives.

Pam is the owner of Crochetpreneur, a business training course and membership for crochet business owners. She had a hat pattern go viral and sold sixteen thousand in a few weeks, which led her to leaving for "day job" as a mental health counselor. She now serves thousands of people in the creative arts, teaching them how to be entrepreneurs and monetize their gifts. Pam also has her own mastermind but was thrilled to join Braver Together Mastermind with us—and her best friend is joining, too!

Melonie is America's Dementia Coach and consults with adult care facilities all over the globe on how to care for residents with her proprietary approach and leadership framework. She also serves individuals with her coaching, guidebook, and resources.

As you can see, the diversity is immense and adds to the value of the community, knowledge, and learning we can glean from the group.

From Transaction to Transformation

As Oprah Winfrey wisely said, "Surround yourself only with people who are going to take you higher." It's not about assembling a group for mutual back-scratching. The community you cultivate within a mastermind should be transformational, lifting you and every member to new heights, breaking barriers, and co-creating a path for unprecedented successes.

Mission Statement and Values of the Group

Often, mastermind groups have a written mission statement, a list of agreed upon values, or maybe even a guiding theme or mantra.

Here is an example:

The Braver Together Mastermind is an intimate mastermind for experienced Christian women entrepreneurs who want to reach their next level of success with boldness, bravery, confidence, and clarity while being well supported within a high-level community of their most aspirational (and inspirational) peers.

Our mantra is: we are #bravertogether

On the next page, you'll find a list of potential values that your mastermind could adopt and agree to. As always, I suggest you make it your own, and I am here to help you when you are ready for private coaching or a Create Your Mastermind VIP day.

A Synergy of Souls

It's not just about the brains—it's also about the heart. Emotional intelligence and empathy become the glue that holds your intellectual prowess together, creating a synergy of souls that enriches the logical and emotional facets of each member. You're not just a "think tank"; you're a "feel and think tank," a communal entity that appreciates the whole human experience.

The synergy between a mastermind group and community is multifaceted and instrumental in optimizing both personal and professional growth.

This is how it works together:

- **Community as Social Capital:** In a mastermind group, community serves as an invaluable form of social capital, providing a network of experts and resources that can expedite problem-solving and innovation.

VALUES OF YOUR MASTERMIND GROUP

When creating a Mastermind group, you might want to co-create a list of VALUES.

Here is a list of potential examples:

1. **Integrity:** Upholding the highest standards of honesty in all actions.

2. **Accountability:** Members are responsible for their own commitments and should hold each other accountable.

3. **Mutual Respect:** Valuing each individual's unique journey, experience, and viewpoint.

4. **Confidentiality:** Safeguarding the privacy and trust within the group.

5. **Personal Growth:** A commitment to continual learning and self-improvement.

6. **Supportive Community:** Building a network that uplifts, teaches, and provides emotional backing.

7. **Action-Oriented:** Ideas are great, but implementation is key.

8. **Transparency:** Openness in sharing successes as well as failures, to foster group learning.

9. **Strategic Focus:** Aim for specific, measurable, attainable, relevant, and timely (SMART) goals.

10. **Spiritual Grounding:** Incorporating spiritual or ethical principles as the foundational building blocks of all interactions and activities.

Each of these values contributes to a balanced and enriching mastermind experience.

Mastermind Moment

from Mary Grant

Let me introduce you to my business partner in crime, Mary Grant.

I met Mary Grant in a Mastermind hosted by Jamie Bright. We live across the world from each other . . . she is in Dublin, Ireland and has been a fashion designer for over 30 years. We became fast friends after meeting in person at our yearly live retreat in Arizona in 2022 and have not stopped in our endless collaborative discussions on Telegram ever since. We have gone on to be in another mastermind together hosted by Cody Burch. We both applied to do a TEDx talk together, and she was chosen and will be speaking live from the Red Circle Stage in just a few months.

We always talk about how we "move mountains" together as we work on projects, website pages, emails, and all things in the entrepreneur world. But I love that we also share a bold vision for women being transformed and often just talk about normal stuff like family dynamics, errands for the day, and even self-care.

"Being in a mastermind has been a game changer for me. For so many years, I was working on my own, trying to figure it all out on my own. I craved community, and then I discovered masterminds. The collective experience of the group shortcuts through so much trail and error. That's also where I met my business bestie. Together, we move mountains every single day."

www.MaryGrant.com

- **Accountability Mechanisms:** A strong community fosters a heightened level of accountability. The group acts as a series of checks and balances, ensuring each member stays committed to their objectives.

- **Collective Intelligence:** The community within a mastermind offers a rich tapestry of diverse perspectives, amplifying the collective intelligence. This leads to more informed decisions and strategies.

- **Knowledge Transfer:** The presence of experienced individuals within the community enables a seamless transfer of tacit knowledge, providing actionable insights that can mitigate risks and elevate success rates.

- **Emotional Resilience:** The intrinsic emotional support provided by a tight-knit community can act as a psychological safety net, enhancing resilience and adaptability in volatile conditions.

- **Celebratory Milestones:** In a mastermind community, successes are not individual but collective. Each milestone achieved is a validation of the community's cumulative effort, enriching the overall experience.

By capitalizing on these facets, your Mastermind group stands to become not just a forum for professional development, but a catalyst for holistic enrichment.

In summary, the quality of your mastermind is directly proportional to the quality of the community that populates it. From my years of curating mastermind groups, I can attest that your investment in fostering a nurturing, dynamic community will yield returns beyond your wildest imagination.

Questions to Ponder on
COMMUNITY

If you are considering JOINING A MASTERMIND:

- What type of mastermind community are you looking for?

- What key components do you desire?

- What types of people do you want to be immersed with?

If you are considering CREATING A MASTERMIND:

- What type of community do you wholeheartedly want to create?

- What are 3-5 key feelings you want your mastermind to have?

- What do you want your mastermind to be "known for"?

ONE INSPIRED IDEA CAN CHANGE *everything*

The *Mastermind* Effect

COMMUNITY

The reason masterminds are effective is the community component for ongoing growth, learning and expansion.

COLLABORATION

Collaborations multiply in a mastermind by nature of the sharing of ideas, resources, experiences and opportunities.

COMMUNICATION

Communication lays a foundation of higher level conversations, about mindset, messaging, marketing and more.

CONSISTENCY

By being together on an ongoing basis, we know each other deeply and remind each other of our strengths, gifts, talents and abilities.

COMMITMENT

With the commitment of a mastermind, you have the gift of transformation and the trust of knowing WE are all here together.

CHAPTER THREE

Cultivate Collaborations

> Alone we can do so little;
> together we can do so much.
>
> HELEN KELLER

What is collaboration?

Collaboration is the act of working together with someone to produce or create something.

Having established the imperative of community, we now turn our attention to the dynamic that fuels it: collaboration. You see, a mastermind is not a spectator sport. Every member must be engaged, actively collaborating to explore solutions, strategize next moves, and optimize outcomes. It's a multidirectional exchange of value, and this chapter aims to decode its complexities.

The Mechanics of Collaboration

Collaboration isn't mere cooperation; it's a symbiotic relationship that elevates every member to a higher plane of performance. It involves setting joint goals, sharing resources, and most importantly, abandoning the zero-sum game mentality. In a collaborative setting, your gain isn't another's loss; it's a collective win that uplifts the group as a whole.

Navigating Differences

If you think collaborating with diverse minds is akin to herding cats, you're missing the point. Different opinions—even conflicts—are not the antithesis to collaboration; they're the catalysts. They offer an opportunity to examine issues from multiple perspectives, fostering a richer, more nuanced understanding that leads to superior decisions.

The Alchemy of Ideas

In my extensive years of leading masterminds, I've found that when collaboration is executed correctly, it creates an alchemy of ideas. A simple concept, when passed through the prism of a mastermind group, can morph into a multi-faceted gem of immense value. It's the hallmark of what I call THE MASTERMIND EFFECT.

Leading with Humility

"The best collaborations create something bigger than the sum of what each person can create on their own," said American writer and philanthropist Melinda Gates. Indeed, the ego has no room in a collaborative setting. Leading with humility allows space for others' ideas and experiences to influence your own, shaping a collective vision that serves individual and communal objectives.

Leveraging Collaboration for Collective Success

Collaboration amplifies individual efforts, fostering innovation and shared success. High-level entrepreneurs embrace collaboration over competition, recognizing that pooling resources, expertise, and insights results in powerful outcomes that surpass individual capabilities.

Key Ideas to Consider:

- Explore opportunities for joint ventures, partnerships, and collaborations.

- Engage with your mastermind group to brainstorm and ideate collectively.

- Share wins, referral sources, technology hacks, and even virtual assistants.

- Leverage the diverse skills and experiences of your network to address challenges.

- Celebrate shared successes as a testament to the power of collaboration.

A Tapestry of Achievement

Networking and collaboration form the tapestry upon which entrepreneurial success is woven. Visionary entrepreneurs understand that nurturing authentic relationships and embracing collaboration yield exponential growth and innovation. By weaving their experiences into the fabric of their networks and mastermind groups, they harness the collective wisdom that propels them towards new heights.

Continuing forward, the MASTERMIND EFFECT explores leadership authenticity, overcoming challenges, innovation, and legacy. Through these principles, entrepreneurs empower themselves to lead with purpose, innovate with impact, and leave a lasting legacy of achievement.

Collaboration isn't an abstract concept; it's an actionable strategy that—when implemented with intentionality and expertise—becomes the driving force of a successful mastermind. In the chapters that follow, you'll gain insights into the tools and techniques that facilitate effective collaboration. But for now, recognize that the act of collaborating is not just a means to an end; it's the essence of the journey itself.

Mastermind Moment

from Marta Spirk

The power of mastermind groups goes beyond its scheduled meetings and can create a web of valuable connections. These connections often manifest as enduring friendships, unwavering support systems, and fruitful collaborations that can span years.

Personally, I've experienced the profound impact of masterminds in nurturing relationships that have enriched both my personal and professional life. One such connection emerged from a mastermind with Diane, who I met during a coaching program. Our synergy was evident, and it was no coincidence that we eventually joined the same mastermind group. In no time, we were exploring opportunities to leverage each other's strengths and expertise for mutual benefit. Diane, with her wealth of knowledge, became a valuable addition to my professional network.

As entrepreneurs, we often underestimate the value of introducing our mastermind peers to our own audience. However, I've discovered that sharing the wisdom and insights of fellow mastermind participants with my clients and network enhances their perception of me. By inviting them to contribute as guest speakers in my podcast episodes and virtual summits, we've created a symbiotic relationship that benefits all parties involved.

In essence, masterminds are not just confined to the duration of the group itself; they are catalysts for lasting connections that continue to nurture personal and professional growth long after the formal meetings have concluded. These connections become a reservoir of support, wisdom, and collaboration, enriching our lives in ways we might never have anticipated.

www.MartaSpirk.com

Questions to Ponder on
COLLABORATION

If you are considering JOINING A MASTERMIND:

- What type of different people would you love to start collaborating with?

- What do you have to OFFER the group that could be helpful to others?

- How could the power of the group impact your future?

If you are considering CREATING A MASTERMIND:

- What types of people would you love to have in your mastermind?

- What types of people are NOT the right fit for your mastermind?

- Write a list of your "wish list" clients that you would love to invite to join your mastermind based on their skills, connections and wisdom.

YOUR WORK IS A

Work of Art

The *Mastermind* Effect

COMMUNITY

The reason masterminds are effective is the community component for ongoing growth, learning and expansion.

COLLABORATION

Collaborations multiply in a mastermind by nature of the sharing of ideas, resources, experiences and opportunities.

COMMUNICATION

Communication lays a foundation of higher level conversations, about mindset, messaging, marketing and more.

CONSISTENCY

By being together on an ongoing basis, we know each other deeply and remind each other of our strengths, gifts, talents and abilities.

COMMITMENT

With the commitment of a mastermind, you have the gift of transformation and the trust of knowing WE are all here together.

CHAPTER FOUR

Cultivate Communication

The single biggest problem with communication is
the illusion that it has taken place.

GEORGE BERNARD SHAW

A fter understanding the nuances of community and collaboration, it's time to tackle the linchpin that holds them together: *communication*.

Don't mistake this for a soft skill; it's a core competency, a mastery over which can make or break the effectiveness of a mastermind.

What exactly is COMMUNICATION?

Communication is the process of sending and receiving messages or information between individuals.

The Double-Edged Sword

The power of communication can't be overstated, but it's a double-edged sword. Excellent communication can catapult a mastermind into the stratosphere of effectiveness, while poor communication can ground it before it even takes off. It's not just about transmitting your thoughts, but also about how you receive, interpret, and respond to those of others.

The Art of Listening

While most of us have been trained to speak clearly, few of us have been taught to listen effectively. Yet, in a mastermind setting, listening is half of the equation. When done correctly, it's a dynamic act that involves not just hearing words but understanding their underlying sentiments, implications, and nuances.

Socratic Dialogue Over Monologues

This isn't the stage for a soliloquy. The richness of a

mastermind comes from back-and-forths, questions, and challenging the status quo. Socratic dialogue, the kind that provokes thought and examines underlying assumptions, is far more valuable than one-sided monologues.

It is more like an improv class. We embrace the "Yes, And" philosophy.

The Transparency Paradigm

Imagine a room where people speak not just with their lips but also with their hearts. That's the level of transparency that a mastermind demands. It requires vulnerability, a willingness to share not just your triumphs but also your fears, challenges, and uncertainties.

Authenticity is the cornerstone of an effective mastermind group. Brave entrepreneurs understand that building genuine connections goes beyond transactional interactions. By fostering authentic relationships based on trust and mutual respect, entrepreneurs create a network that offers insights, support, and opportunities.

Effective Tools and Platforms

In this digital age, multiple platforms can facilitate communication within a mastermind. From Voxer or Telegram channels to Facebook groups to digital classrooms, technology can enhance—not impede—interpersonal communications, provided it is chosen and employed judiciously.

In my mastermind group, this has been such a game-changing addition. We have a Voxer channel for questions, hotseats on the go, emotional support, and cheering each other on as we take bold steps. A place to have "the meeting in between the meetings" and dive deeper by hearing each other's voices, and sharing a quick photo or even a funny GIF. It helps the group get to know you in a more intimate way if you fully engage in the opportunity.

Hosting live events for your mastermind can be a magnifying multiplier as people get to sit in rooms together. The brainstorming, fun, laughter, and hugs are unprecedented as we have time to talk "officially" and then magic that happens in the conversations at the coffee stand or over dinner.

All of these combined are what knits a group together in ways that cannot be measured financially. We become kindred spirits.

Masterful communication turns a mastermind from a disparate group of individuals into a coherent, focused entity. It sets the stage for breakthroughs and transformations that are inconceivable in its absence. As we progress, we will delve into the practicalities—of consistency, commitment, and the power of curiosity. For now, understand this: effective communication is not optional; it's imperative.

Mastermind Moment

from Paula Tobey

The Transformative Impact of the Braver Together Mastermind

Hey there, I'm Paula, and I can't even begin to tell you how the Braver Together Mastermind has shaped my entrepreneurial journey. Trust me, the importance of a supportive peer group is like the hidden gem in a treasure chest of success.

The Evolution of Goal Setting and Achievements

I've dabbled in other masterminds before, but let me tell you, this one? It's the real deal. The "hot seat" and roundtable discussions have honestly opened my mind in ways I didn't think possible. It's like going from a casual jog to a sprint—I've felt a real shift in my mindset and actions.

Problem-Solving through Collective Intelligence

Obstacles and challenges? Oh, they've knocked on my door more than once. But the collective brainpower in this mastermind is like having an army of wisdom warriors. We pull together, dissect the challenge, and boom! Solutions appear like magic.

Networking as a Valuable Resource

In today's business game, who you know can make all the difference. The Braver Together Mastermind is a Facebook group on steroids, but with real connections. It's already paid off; I've found some super exciting opportunities for my podcasting project.

Alleviating the Solitude of Solopreneurship

Being a solopreneur has its perks, but let's be real—it can get lonely. This mastermind is my go-to squad. It's a safe space where I can share, ask for feedback, and just breathe easier knowing I'm not in this alone.

Skill Enhancement and Personal Growth

While I haven't exactly become a tech wizard overnight, the growth in my perspectives has been off the charts. When you're feeling stuck, a room full of varying viewpoints is like the ultimate cheat code for breaking out of your shell.

So, if you're on the lookout for a space that offers more than just the same ol' advice and awkward interactions, then you've got to check out the Braver Together Mastermind. I love the way Diane paves the way to help us step up into the next version of ourselves!

Trust me, if you're seeking a circle of empowered women committed to elevating each other, then this is your ticket to a fulfilling and successful entrepreneurial life.

paulatobey.com

Questions to Ponder on
COMMUNICATION

If you are considering JOINING A MASTERMIND:

- What type of communication do you desire from the group? Ongoing? Weekly Zoom meetings? Live events a few times a year?

- Are you ready (and willing) to enhance your vulnerability by sharing freely in the group to get support and also provide value?

- Do you want a small group or a larger group dynamic?

If you are considering CREATING A MASTERMIND:

- How often do you want to host the meetings?

- What do you want for the length of commitment and the level of transparency?

- Do you want to include any private coaching options for your members as a bonus or at a discounted rate while they are enrolled?

BE REAL

ASK FOR HELP

Take action

The *Mastermind* Effect

COMMUNITY
The reason masterminds are effective is the community component for ongoing growth, learning and expansion.

COLLABORATION
Collaborations multiply in a mastermind by nature of the sharing of ideas, resources, experiences and opportunities.

COMMUNICATION
Communication lays a foundation of higher level conversations, about mindset, messaging, marketing and more.

CONSISTENCY
By being together on an ongoing basis, we know each other deeply and remind each other of our strengths, gifts, talents and abilities.

COMMITMENT
With the commitment of a mastermind, you have the gift of transformation and the trust of knowing WE are all here together.

CHAPTER FIVE

Cultivate Consistency

Small disciplines repeated with consistency
very day lead to great achievements
gained slowly over time.

JOHN C. MAXWELL

After exploring curating in all its glory, it's time to pivot to a principle that often gets overshadowed: consistency. This chapter hones in on why consistent actions, however small, can yield big rewards in the realm of masterminds.

What is CONSISTENCY?

Consistency refers to the quality of achieving a level

of performance over time that doesn't vary greatly.

Consistency: The Backbone of Progress

As the old adage goes, "Rome wasn't built in a day." Achieving meaningful progress requires steady, consistent effort. In a mastermind group, consistency plays a crucial role in maintaining the momentum generated by the members. Regular meetings, sustained commitment, and dependable follow-through are necessary for the group to realize both its short-term objectives and long-term aspirations.

The Snowball Effect

The power of consistency lies in its ability to compound over time. Think of each consistent action as a snowball rolling down a hill, gathering more and more snow (or in this case, success) as it goes.

My Braver Together Mastermind has key members that keep coming back year after year as alumni. This gives the group a consistent core of knowledge and a legacy of consistent transformational relationships.

The Consistency-Trust Equation

Consistency is instrumental in building trust within

the group. When everyone shows up and contributes regularly, it creates a stable environment where vulnerability and innovation can thrive.

As we get to know each other on Zoom calls and in the Voxer channel, we become deeply integrated and then the times together in person magnify the mastermind experience with the level of vulnerability and fun adventures that can only happen in person.

Consistency in Quality

Let's get it straight—consistency is not about becoming a robot that churns out tasks. It's about maintaining a high standard of quality in your contributions and interactions. Consistency in quality leads to collective elevation, setting the stage for breakthroughs.

For the mastermind I run and the ones I am a part of, it is important to attend the meetings. They are on my calendar and I am committed to being there unless I am traveling or there is an emergency. It is the give and take of "being a part of," not a selfish stance of "what's in it for me?" Without fail, every meeting I attend, I learn something from every person's share or hotseat.

Beating the Odds with Consistency

The difference between a failed and a flourishing mastermind often boils down to consistency. It's the "slow and steady" principle; it may not offer the instant gratification of a quick win, but it stands the test of time.

This is a marathon, not a sprint. That is the power of THE MASTERMIND EFFECT. We are not in a one-time workshop together. We are together for a long commitment of time and often years of working together as a group.

The Rhythm of Consistency

Consistency is not just about repetition; it's about establishing a rhythm. This rhythm becomes the heartbeat of the mastermind, setting a pace that makes it easier for everyone to stay in sync and move toward collective goals.

The routines of the group become the lasting impression and legacy. Be ready for your life to change as you go deeper into the experience of a true mastermind.

Let me share a few examples:

Heather has been a key member of my Braver Together Mastermind. She has journeyed with us through the evolution of owning a Box Company, to starting her Marketing Agency, to now being the newest President and CEO of the National Association of Christian Women Entrepreneurs (NACWE). All while getting support from the group.

Stephanie has learned how to expand her 25-year counseling career and go virtual with digital courses, workshops, and online trainings. She has been with us as an alumni for years.

Heidi has expanded her coaching practice and created her signature course, A Season of Me, and been supported by the Braver Together Mastermind girls as she added a new book series, a podcast, and church facilitation to her offer suite.

Consistency may not be the most glamorous concept, but its impact is undeniable. It's the glue that holds all the other principles together, transforming the chaotic potential of a group of individuals into the harmonious reality of a transformative mastermind.

Mastermind Moment

from Heidi Kleine

The Transformative Power of Masterminds

Heidi is a long-term member of the Braver Together Mastermind. She is a coach who works with women pursuing their calls, pastors, churches, and leaders. She believes in the leadership of women and calls herself a Christian Feminist.

Heidi notes the unparalleled level of accountability she's experienced since joining the mastermind. "The most valuable aspect of the mastermind is the community. It's an unusual environment where you can be inspired and share things you might not be able to share in your normal day-to-day life." With the support of the mastermind, Heidi has committed to and achieved several crucial milestones, including creating her signature course, book, and podcast: A Season of Me.

"The mastermind has meant that I have written down my goals. The group encourages me and also reminds me about what I said I was planning to do." The Braver Together Mastermind functions as a dynamic sounding board where we hold one another accountable for our bigger vision. Far from a wish list, these are goals written, verbalized, and then pursued with the collective energy of the group.

The power of community in a mastermind group is its unique value. By facilitating an environment where like-minded individuals share their aspirations and challenges, it creates a circle of trust and inspiration.

Mastermind groups often serve as a support system during personal challenges, such as those related to relationships. The focus is not on wallowing but on constructive problem-solving. Heidi said, "We are here for you when you need a place to say, 'Yeah, this is hard.' It's not about quitting; it's about asking 'how do we' solve the things that are happening."

A collateral benefit of a mastermind is the skill enhancement it provides. Participants aren't just learning from their own experiences but also from the diverse skill sets of other members. It's a cross-pollination for personal development and coaching expansion. "Being a part of a mastermind has really expanded my coaching skills. I get to see how other people in the group facilitate coaching."

"Sometimes just showing up in the mastermind meeting is the difference. It enables me to stay focused on my business and propels it forward." For me, the act of showing up—both physically and mentally—can, at times, be the game-changer. It serves as a psychological reset, reinvigorating members and helping me regain focus on my business goals.

Heidi's journey through the Braver Together Mastermind illustrates a multidimensional transformation, not just in her business but in her life's broader tapestry. It's a testament to the power of community, accountability, and yes, the relentless magic of simply showing up, and becoming more and more her authentic self.

www.heidikleine.com

Questions to Ponder on CONSISTENCY

If you are considering JOINING A MASTERMIND:

- Are you willing to consistently show up to be a contributing member?

- Are you open to feedback and support?

- Will you engage in the conversation in the Voxer, Telegram or Facebook group in between meetings to be a vibrant member?

If you are considering CREATING A MASTERMIND:

- What do you want your members to consistently do?

- Are you ready to commit for the ongoing journey?

- What fears rise up in you about this longer-term offer?

IT'S MORE THAN ONE DAY AT A TIME

It's one Brave at a time

The *Mastermind* Effect

COMMUNITY

The reason masterminds are effective is the community component for ongoing growth, learning and expansion.

COLLABORATION

Collaborations multiply in a mastermind by nature of the sharing of ideas, resources, experiences and opportunities.

COMMUNICATION

Communication lays a foundation of higher level conversations, about mindset, messaging, marketing and more.

CONSISTENCY

By being together on an ongoing basis, we know each other deeply and remind each other of our strengths, gifts, talents and abilities.

COMMITMENT

With the commitment of a mastermind, you have the gift of transformation and the trust of knowing WE are all here together.

CHAPTER SIX

Cultivate Commitment

Until one is committed, there is hesitancy,
the chance to draw back.

JOHANN WOLFGANG VON GOETHE

What is commitment?

Commitment is the state or quality of being dedicated to a cause or activity.

If community is the backbone and collaboration its muscle, then commitment is undoubtedly the lifeblood of a successful mastermind. For this collaborative edifice to stand and thrive, each individual must invest not just their time and expertise, but also a genuine commitment to collective growth.

You can have all the talent and intelligence in the world, but without commitment, a mastermind is but a hollow echo chamber. This chapter serves as a call-to-action, urging each member to fully invest in the mastermind process—because a committed group can literally change lives.

Punctuality: The First Step

We'll kick off with something as seemingly simple as showing up on time. This is the first indicator of commitment and sets the stage for the quality of interactions that follow. It's a gesture of respect, not only for the time of others but also for the transformative process you've all committed to.

Skill Contribution: The Unique Flavor

Every person in a mastermind brings a unique set of skills and perspectives. Being committed means not holding back; it's contributing your expertise and insights actively to create a rich, diversified collective intelligence. You're not just a seat filler; you're a key ingredient in this recipe for success.

In my Braver Together Mastermind, we often invite

members to teach on a subject. I also love to feature them on my podcast and in blogs that showcase them for my audience. We have also written books together, and I am adding their insights into this book.

The Ripple Effect of Commitment

When everyone in the room is fully invested, the energy is palpable. Each person's commitment acts as a catalyst, elevating the group's collective output. The result? Breakthroughs that have the power to change lives—yours and those you influence.

The commitment in my Braver Together Mastermind has led to the women hosting events together, being on each other's podcasts, supporting each other in private conversations, and often referring to each other or even buying each other's programs/offers, as desired.

Making Commitment Actionable

Let's get pragmatic here. Commitment is not a vague, lofty ideal; it needs to be made actionable. This means having a clear code of conduct, a set of responsibilities, and consequences for not meeting them. When commitment is tangible, it's easier to measure and uphold.

We commit to each other, the group, confidentiality, and ongoing transformation.

Life-Changing Potential

"Commitment leads to action. Action brings your dream closer," said American businesswoman Marcia Wieder. Indeed, in a mastermind, your commitment doesn't just serve you; it serves the collective dream of the group. When everyone is committed, the potential for life-altering insights, breakthroughs, and transformations becomes not just possible, but probable.

Commitment is the fuel that powers the mastermind engine. It's what elevates a group from a casual meeting of minds to a life-changing force to be reckoned with. From showing up on time to actively contributing your unique skills, each act of commitment is a vital thread in the fabric of a transformative mastermind experience.

Commitment also provides us with confidence and clarity, as we journey together over the months and years. We get ongoing awareness and feedback.

Commitment to my own journey also opens the door to confidence. I am committed to my business, to the group, and to us, and often we can "borrow confidence." For me, this means that "brave begets brave." By being with other people doing brave acts in business, it rubs off on me and I gain courage. That is why I changed the name of my mastermind to the Braver Together Mastermind in Fall of 2022.

Confidence is not just a trait; it's a dynamic force that propels individuals and groups towards success. Within a mastermind setting, confidence enables participants to voice their opinions, share their expertise, and take calculated risks. By fostering a space where each member feels validated and respected, the group taps into a powerful reservoir of collective confidence, amplifying its overall potential for success.

Clarity: The Guiding Star

Confidence then allows me to step into clarity. The power of the mastermind is SEEING myself through the eyes of others.

"You can't read the label on the bottle" is a saying I've heard recently. I can't see my own gifts, talents, and abilities but the mastermind group can mirror them back to me. They can also remind me that the ups and downs of the clarity cycle are normal.

Navigating the complexities of entrepreneurship is akin to sailing in uncharted waters. Clarity serves as the compass, guiding the group's focus and deci-

The *Clarity* Cycle

We move from **chaos** and **confusion** to **CLARITY**. Often. Daily. Hourly. Weekly.

We mistakenly believe that this means we are off-track or not smart enough.

It is simply the normal process of entrepreneurship, learning and life.

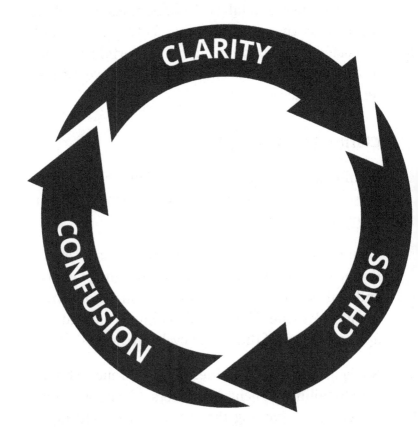

sion-making processes. A well-defined set of goals and objectives provides a roadmap for the group, allowing for effective planning and efficient use of resources. It ensures that each member's efforts align with the collective vision, enabling the group to steer clear of distractions and setbacks.

Beyond Signed Contracts and Handshakes

While formal agreements and protocols are essential, the real commitment transcends ink and paper. It's an internal pledge to contribute meaningfully, to approach each session with an open mind and the unquenchable thirst to improve—both personally and as a collective.

The Currency of Trust

When each member is genuinely committed, trust proliferates. This isn't trivial; trust is the currency of any successful mastermind. In a space brimming with trust, people feel secure sharing their ideas, challenges, and dreams, thereby enriching the entire experience.

Intermittent vs. Sustained Commitment

Dabbling isn't an option. Commitment must be sustained over the long haul, carried through the ebbs and flows of motivation, past the inevitable challenges and disappointments. It's this unyielding commitment that differentiates a mastermind from a casual brainstorming session.

Accountability Mechanisms

Let's be real; even the most committed can waver. That's where accountability mechanisms come into play. Whether it's an accountability partner within the group or periodic progress check-ins, these systems help keep commitment levels high.

The Power of Consistency

As the famous entrepreneur and motivational speaker, Marie Forleo, once said, "Consistency is not really about discipline; it is about becoming the person you want to be." Consistency in commitment manifests through regular participation, meaningful contributions, and ongoing effort—not just in high-stakes situations but in every interaction, big or small.

Commitment is the invisible thread that weaves together the diverse tapestry of a mastermind group. Without it, even the most brilliant ensemble is just a gathering of smart individuals. With it, the group transforms into a dynamic, evolving entity capable of producing exponential growth and change.

Mastermind Moment

from Noelle D'Intino

For years, I have been a member of various masterminds. What truly makes them unique is the diversity within the groups. People are at different stages in their lives, entrepreneurial paths, and come with a variety of experiences. That adds many extraordinary dynamics to our discussions. I love hearing the perspective of someone just starting out versus someone on version number eight of their business.

My involvement in masterminds has brought immense value to my professional endeavors and all aspects of my life, personal and business alike. I consistently walk away from our meetings with precious nuggets of innovative ideas, invaluable insights, fresh perspectives, and, my personal favorite, those pivotal mindset shifts that arrive when I need them most.

Two things that I learned along the way that have significantly impacted the value I receive from being a member of a mastermind is to show up and have something to share about yourself. You are part of a group to get an experience, and you want to show up to get support in whatever you need.

Grab a small notebook, or commit to documenting this in your notes on your phone, and have one of them readily available to you ALWAYS. As I go about my week, living life and encountering various challenges and inspirations, I note any topics or issues I'd like to bring to my mastermind group. This simple practice has transformed my mastermind experience, giving me a readily available list of discussion points to brainstorm, seek ideas, gain support, or address whatever needs attention. It's a small change that has made a big difference in how I engage with my mastermind group and get the maximum value of our collective wisdom.

Questions to Ponder on COMMITMENT

If you are considering JOINING A MASTERMIND:

- Are you willing to commit?

- Are you open to the new clarity from long-term investment?

- Will you be a committed member of the group?

If you are considering CREATING A MASTERMIND:

- What is the length of your mastermind?

- How long are the meetings?

- What happens if someone wants to drop out?

YOUR CLIENTS WANT THE

evolution

OF YOU

The *Mastermind* Effect

COMMUNITY

The reason masterminds are effective is the community component for ongoing growth, learning and expansion.

COLLABORATION

Collaborations multiply in a mastermind by nature of the sharing of ideas, resources, experiences and opportunities.

COMMUNICATION

Communication lays a foundation of higher level conversations, about mindset, messaging, marketing and more.

CONSISTENCY

By being together on an ongoing basis, we know each other deeply and remind each other of our strengths, gifts, talents and abilities.

COMMITMENT

With the commitment of a mastermind, you have the gift of transformation and the trust of knowing WE are all here together.

CHAPTER SEVEN

The Curated Plan for Cultivation

So, now you have the framework for your MASTERMIND . . . what's next? Our job as leaders of current or future masterminds is to cultivate growth. We want to CURATE and CULTIVATE.

CURATE

To *curate* means to select, organize, and present

something, usually content, for people to use or enjoy.

CULTIVATE

To *cultivate* is to try to acquire or develop (a quality, sentiment, or skill). It usually means to foster growth or improve something, often relationships or skill sets.

We want to create a flourishing ecosystem of success. This chapter decodes the importance of intentional and sustained effort to grow both as individuals and as a collective.

Seeds Don't Grow Overnight

In the realm of masterminds, patience is not just a virtue; it's a requirement. Success won't happen overnight. Cultivation is about acknowledging this and putting in the consistent work necessary to achieve long-term growth.

Personal Growth Fuels Collective Growth

The better you are, the better the group gets. It's not just about capitalizing on what you already know; it's about pushing yourself to acquire new skills, perspectives, and understandings that you can then bring back into the collective pool of wisdom.

The Power of Mentoring

Let's lean into something beyond the group dynamic for a moment: the role of mentorship. Mentorship within a mastermind serves as a powerhouse for rapid cultivation, both for the mentor and the mentee.

Stepping beyond commitment, let's dig into the idea of curating—a word often associated with museums, but equally applicable to a thriving mastermind. It's all about thoughtfully selecting, organizing, and presenting, not just information, but experiences, opportunities, and even relationships.

The Curatorial Mindset

In a world awash with information, what sets a mastermind group apart is its curated quality. This is the intentional act of filtering out the noise to focus on what truly matters. The curatorial mindset shapes not just the content but the context in which interactions occur.

Curating Knowledge

It's not enough to merely share knowledge; the real art lies in curating high-impact insights, tailored to the needs and objectives of the group. This involves discernment, requiring you to sift through vast fields of information to offer up only the most impactful gems.

Curating Interactions

The relationships within a mastermind are not accidental; they are curated. This means carefully selecting participants, fostering meaningful dialogues, and orchestrating interactions that lead to deep connections and potent outcomes.

Curating Opportunities

Being part of a mastermind is also about curating opportunities for each other—whether that's business partnerships, creative collaborations, or chances for personal growth. It's about seeing the potential for alignment and acting on it.

Curating Accountability

Not all forms of accountability are created equal. In a mastermind, the accountability structures are curated to fit the unique composition and objectives of the group. This ensures everyone is held to a standard that is both challenging and achievable.

Curating is an ongoing, thoughtful process that elevates a mastermind from a casual gathering to a highly impactful experience. From the knowledge

THE CURATED MASTERMIND INCLUDES:

Starting Phase:
- Transition from the honeymoon phase to long-term engagement.
- Think of relationship strategy as a guide.

Reliability: The Rhythm and Routines
- Set a predictable meeting schedule.
- Foster trust and accountability through consistency.

Dynamic Fluidity: Engineering Enthusiasm
- Introduce guest experts for fresh insights.
- Use thematic agendas or change meeting formats to avoid monotony.

Member Dynamics: The Science of Adding New Blood
- Have an onboarding process for new members.
- Make newcomers feel integral, not optional.

Measuring Triumphs: The KPIs of Group Genius
- Define and track Key Performance Indicators (KPIs).
- Celebrate financial and career milestones as group achievements.

Conflict Mitigation: The Art of Drama-Free Discourse
- Establish a clear protocol for conflict resolution.
- Aim for empathetic, structured approaches to disagreements.

Face-to-Face Connection: The Power of Physical Presence
- Schedule in-person meetups if geography allows.
- Recognize the high ROI of face-to-face interaction.

Year-End Assessments: Reflect, Recalibrate, and Relaunch
- Conduct an annual review of group performance.
- Use this time to recalibrate goals and recommit to the group.

Milestone Celebrations: Because Every Win Counts
- Celebrate special meetings and milestone achievements.
- Use these occasions to strengthen group bonds and morale.

Ongoing Transformation: Keep Coming Back
- Understand that long-lasting masterminds require strategic intent.
- Emphasize the importance of variety and mutual support.

shared to the relationships fostered, curation enriches every aspect of the group's journey, setting the stage for both immediate impact and long-term transformation.

Feedback Loops: Your New Best Friend

In the process of cultivation, regular feedback loops serve as invaluable signposts. They not only provide a reality check but also offer constructive criticism and commendation, both of which are crucial for growth.

Nurturing Relationships

Beyond professional and personal growth, the relationships you cultivate within the group will often outlive the mastermind itself. Investing in these relationships is as much about the future as it is about the present moment.

Cultivation is the underpinning of all we've discussed so far. It's the quiet, behind-the-scenes work that turns the potential energy of a committed, collaborative, and communicative group into the kinetic energy of real-world success and change.

Mastermind Moment

from Karen Truesdell-Bierman

How Karen Bierman Transformed Her Life and Business Through the Braver Together Mastermind

Dr. Karen Truesdell-Bierman is a Licensed Psychologist who consults with mental health experts and attorneys. While she was content in her career, she felt stagnant and confined to her own perspectives. Traditional consultation and supervision were not pushing her out of her comfort zone.

Enter the Braver Together Mastermind, a transformative experience that broke down Karen's mental walls. The group has provided her with the tools and perspectives she needed to take her business and personal life to the next level. She wasn't just gaining skills; she was gaining a whole new mindset. She has been a member of the group for many years, as she keeps coming back as an ongoing alumni.

Here is what Karen has experienced as a result of being in the Braver Together Mastermind:

1. Enhanced Networking: Karen expanded her network beyond her traditional circles, engaging with entrepreneurs from various industries. This broadened her perspectives and added value to her own profession.

2. Personal Growth: Participating in the mastermind not only elevated Karen's business acumen but also contributed to her personal growth, helping her assimilate valuable life principles from the 12-steps that Diane often shares from her own experience.

3. Shift in Mindset: Initially discouraged by failed marketing ventures, Karen learned to reframe these as gifts to the world—shifting from a mindset of loss to one of generosity and long-term gain.

4. Value of Synergy: For Karen, the group's synergy was invaluable. She particularly appreciated the peer-teaching aspect, where members collectively shared insights and knowledge.

5. Life Transformation: The ripple effects were profound. The principles and skills Karen acquired permeated every aspect of her life, from her professional decisions to her personal boundaries and attitude.

Karen's Final Thoughts:

"The Braver Together Mastermind hasn't just improved my business; it's revolutionized how I approach life. From the 12-steps to the mastermind activities, every facet has been a journey of transformation. I've become more positive, accountable, and clear about my unique gift to the world."

karenctruesdellphd.com

Questions to Ponder on CULTIVATION

If you are considering JOINING A MASTERMIND:

- What skills do you want to attain by being in the mastermind?

- What mindsets do you want to up-level with this group of business owners?

- Why now?

If you are considering CREATING A MASTERMIND:

- How can you keep your group fresh and vibrant?

- What unique options do you want to add that could enhance the mastermind members ongoing learning?

- How can you surprise and delight the members?

Connect

Create

Collaborate

BONUS!

CHAPTER EIGHT

The Curiosity Quotient

> Curiosity will conquer fear
> even more than bravery will.
>
> JAMES STEPHENS

C uriosity is a strong desire to know or learn something. Just when you thought you'd reached the end, here comes a curveball—a delightful detour into the world of curiosity.

This bonus chapter aims to show you why an inquisitive mindset is the cherry on top of your mastermind sundae.

The Alchemy of Curiosity: Turning Questions into Gold

Ah, curiosity—the unsung hero of innovation and progress! Picture this: a room full of mastermind members on Zoom or in person at a retreat. But what's that magical element that elevates the conversation from good to "whoa, did we just crack the code of life?" You guessed it: curiosity.

Curiosity isn't just the difference between a stale brainstorming session and an electrifying one; it's the rocket fuel for your entire entrepreneurial journey. Remember how Einstein got us thinking about relativity? A question about a moving train. Steve Jobs and the iPhone? He questioned why our phones weren't as smart as we were. The transformative power of "what if?" and "why not?" can change the trajectory of businesses and lives.

So, why do some mastermind groups fizzle while others sizzle? Simple: the level of collective curiosity. When everyone is eager to explore, question, and challenge the status quo, you're not just brainstorming; you're storming the castle of mediocrity!

Curiosity creates an intoxicating feedback loop. One brilliant question leads to an answer, which leads to another brilliant question. Before you know it, you've all but forgotten about your coffee, and you're discovering solutions you didn't even know you were seeking. That's the alchemy of curiosity: turning questions into gold.

Curiosity: The Eternal Flame

Think of curiosity as the eternal flame that never goes out. It's the driving force that keeps you asking, "what if?" and "why not?" It's the matchstick that ignites new ideas and turns stagnation into innovation.

Curiosity Fuels Collaboration

Ever noticed how the most productive mastermind sessions are buzzing with questions? That's because curiosity is contagious. It fuels collaboration, taking conversations from surface-level to, "Wow, I never thought of it that way!"

Get Uncomfortable: The Growth Zone

Curiosity often pushes you into areas you're unfamiliar with—and that's a good thing! Being a little uncomfortable is a sign that you're in the growth zone. It's where you expand your capabilities, discover new perspectives, and unlock the full potential of the mastermind.

The Curiosity-Resilience Connection

Life is going to throw curveballs; that's a given. However, a curious mindset helps you look beyond the immediate setback and discover the lesson behind it. In this way, curiosity breeds resilience, enabling you to bounce back stronger every time.

Curiosity as a Catalyst for Change

Whether it's personal transformation or making waves in your industry, curiosity is often the catalyst for change. It's what propels you to challenge the status quo, to look beyond the obvious, and to envision a future filled with endless possibilities.

If masterminds were a potion, curiosity would be that secret ingredient that makes everything come alive. It adds depth, color, and a sense of adventure to your journey, ensuring that you're not just going through the motions but truly evolving along the way.

Mastermind Moment

from Michelle Sandler

Diane is not just a business associate; she is someone who has been an integral part of my personal and professional growth journey. Our connection was forged through our shared experiences in not one, but two mastermind groups, as well as a near-death experience in a car accident with a semi-truck. Diane has had a profound impact on my life.

Our journey together in these mastermind groups has been nothing short of transformative. Diane possesses a unique ability to inspire, motivate, and guide, making her an exceptional partner in the pursuit of personal and professional excellence. Through the power of masterminds, we have embarked on a collaborative path of discovery, learning, and achievement.

What sets Diane apart is her unwavering commitment to the success and growth of everyone in our mastermind groups. She has consistently been a source of encouragement, offering insightful perspectives, practical advice, and a listening ear when needed most. Our collaborative efforts have not only elevated our individual pursuits but have also strengthened the bonds of friendship and trust between us.

Our experiences together have been a testament to the incredible power of mastermind groups in fostering meaningful relationships. The camaraderie, mutual support, and shared goals we have cultivated have enriched both our personal and professional lives. Through the ups and downs, we have celebrated successes and navigated challenges together, emerging stronger and more resilient each time.

The accident with the semi-truck was a pivotal moment in our journey. It tested our mettle and reinforced our bond as we faced adversity head-on. It serves as a reminder of the resilience we share and the unwavering support we provide each other, not just in the world of business but in every aspect of life.

As Diane continues to share her insights and wisdom gleaned from hosting masterminds, I have no doubt that her work will be a source of inspiration to countless others. Her dedication to helping people harness the endless possibilities created in mastermind groups is a testament to her passion and expertise in this field.

www.shellcreative.org

Questions to Ponder on CURIOSITY

If you are considering JOINING A MASTERMIND:

- What questions do you want to ask the facilitator?

- What questions do you want to ask the members?

- Why are you willing to invest the time, energy, and money?

If you are considering CREATING A MASTERMIND:

- What is your next step to get your mastermind launched?

- Do you want my help?

- Are you ready to set up a call or book a Create Your Mastermind VIP Day?

Repetition
IS A GIFT

Afterword

> Authenticity is the daily practice of letting go
> of who we think we're supposed to be
> and embracing who we are.
>
> BRENÉ BROWN

As you can see, I am in love with what happens in a mastermind. I am the "Queen of Masterminds," and it is the very favorite thing I do in my offer suite.

I hope you leave inspired.

I hope you embrace the simple, yet profound concepts of THE MASTERMIND EFFECT.

I hope you choose to take the next step by joining one or creating your own.

My biggest desire is that you take bold brave action as an entrepreneur as you follow your crazy dreams!

Mastermind Moment

from Diane Cunningham Ellis

In May 2023, I went to attend a live three-day event in Colorado Springs with two of my friends that I met in one mastermind. It was hosted by Cody Burch, who had been a guest expert and had come to speak to my other mastermind group at our retreat in April that was held in Wisconsin.

Mary came from Ireland, Michelle arrived from the Washington, D.C. area, and I came from Dallas, Texas.

Upon arriving, our plan was to go to dinner and get settled in before our three-day event. Instead, as we were driving to our dinner, we got into a car accident where our rental car was hit by a semi-truck. We all ended up being physically fine, but the rental car was NOT. What happened over the next few days as we processed this event turned us into a life-long mini-mastermind group, which we lovingly call Semi-Survivor Sisters, and the three of us ended up joining this new mastermind group together.

We now have the entire group of nine and then our smaller group of three to get input, feedback, support, and business transformation. So, what was a frightening experience turned into a testimony of triumph.

The immense support of the group was life affirming. And the first person that I told about this accident was (of course) my husband, but then I immediately went to the Voxer channel for my Braver Together Mastermind to ask for their prayers, love, and support.

This is why the mantra of my group and my life message is that we are #bravertogether

THE THREE OF US AT THE GARDEN OF THE GODS IN COLORADO SPRINGS

WAYS TO
Work with Me

My track record of successfully helping small business owners and entrepreneurs create more profitable businesses spans 18 years, starting in 2005. Prior to that, I was working as a Mental Health Counselor since 1997. Over the years, I have helped thousands of dreamers create dreams and own their magnificence.

I am honored to walk this path with visionary, high-achieving women and men who are ready to scale their businesses.

Today, I offer three distinct opportunities to work with me for forward thinking action-taking business builders. Each of them gives you direct access to my 25 years of experience as a coach, consultant, and former counselor and provides you with a unique package of benefits.

Opportunity #1: Braver Together Mastermind
Opportunity #2: Private Coaching and VIP Days
Opportunity #3: Voxer Coaching

On the next few pages, you can read more about each of these ways we can work together to grow your influence, business, and profits.

To find out more visit:
www.DianeCunningham.com

The Braver Together Mastermind is the exclusive mastermind for experienced Christian women entrepreneurs who want to reach their next level of success with boldness, bravery, confidence, and clarity while being well supported within a high-level community of their most aspirational (and inspirational) peers.

It is a six-month commitment, but most women stay on for years to continue the deep relationships and keep the momentum. It includes access to all of my courses and any new offers that I create during your enrollment, for FREE. We also have a Mastermind Voxer Channel, two LIVE 2.5-day retreats each year, and weekly meetings for hotseats, training, and accountability.

To get started, visit the webpage below and fill out the application, or we can set up a call, if you prefer.

www.DianeCunningham.com/Mastermind

Apply today!

Private Coaching and VIP Days

For 18-plus years, I have offered coaching, consulting, and advisory services to high-level entrepreneurs who want the fast track to success without a group dynamic. This is curated to fit your desires and can be as short as a VIP Day or as long as a year. I also have Unlimited Coaching available that includes Voxer Coaching.

If you want specific help, I also have a Create Your Mastermind VIP day where we will dive into the logistics to get yours planned and a timeline for launching.

As my private client, you receive direct access and support to meet your needs and glean from my expertise and experience.

The types of services I provide private clients include things like:

- *Launching your course*
- *Creating a book*
- *Adding Voxer Coaching to your offer suite*
- *Launching an association*
- *Review of marketing materials*
- *Brainstorming and idea sharing*
- *Vendor and recommended resources*
- *Mindset shifts for success*
- *And collaboration ideas*

Go to my website to see my current options (www.dianecunningham.com) or email to get a private curated coaching quote at diane@dianecunningham.com.

Diane Cunningham Ellis   Wed 4:20
✓ Oh good!!!

Starred
◄ Audio Message

voxer

Voxer Coaching

Asynchronous coaching for support without one more appointment. If you want a "coach in your pocket" for quick tips, accountability, strategy, and in the daily brainstorming of ideas, this is for you.

We talk daily in our private channel or as needed. This format opens up options so that you no longer need to fit me in; I am just along the path with you as you build your business, make your offers, and create lasting change.

Voxer is a free walkie talkie app that allows us to communicate and share links, photos, and videos to unlock the unlimited power of conversations. I have found that with my Voxer coaching clients, we go deeper much faster due to the power of what we say and having tiny connection points along the way, without waiting for our next "official session."

Go to my website to see my current options (www. dianecunningham.com) or email to get a private curated coaching quote at diane@dianecunningham.com.

About Diane

Diane Cunningham Ellis, M.Ed. is a "renaissance woman" who lives with her heart on her sleeve and a permanent smile on her face.

She creates. She is a cheerleader to all those she meets. She is a creativity coach, a pied piper of people, a woman of vulnerability, and a passionate heart artist.

She loves to provide women with opportunities to go on brave adventures near and far. She coaches women (and a few brave men) on business, life, recovery, authentic living, and so much more.

She coaches. Diane is a Mastermind Coach, former therapist, plane crash survivor, author, consultant, speaker, marathon runner and fun friend.

She leads. She has a Master's Degree in Education (Guidance and Counseling) from Whitworth College in Spokane, Washington, as well as a Bachelor's Degree in Interpersonal Communications.

She is the Founder of the National Association of Christian Women Entrepreneurs®, a global association where women meet to connect, create, and collaborate. NACWE offers training, conferences, networking, and business strategies. NACWE was launched in May 2010 and has been building and expanding since that time with members through- out the United States and

Canada. She served as President for seven years (2010-2017) and now is a proud member and trusted advisor.

She writes. Diane is the author of twelve books and counting, five which are Amazon Bestsellers, including The Inspired Business Toolkit and the Rock Bottom is a Beautiful Place book series.

She laughs. She currently lives in the Dallas, Texas area. Her house looks like a bookstore, art gallery and office supply store merged. She is messy and has learned to embrace her glorious mess.

She loves. Diane is a heart girl and loves people relentlessly. She gives, she serves, she loves bravely. She is happily married to Jim, her very own Private Investigator, and proudly loves being called Grandma by a few little people.

DIANE@DIANECUNNINGHAM.COM

DIANECUNNINGHAM.COM

FACEBOOK.COM/DIANECUNNINGHAM

FACEBOOK.COM/DIANECUNNINGHAMFRIENDS

Other Books by
Diane Cunningham Ellis

Brave Women Connect

The Inspired Business Toolkit

Inspiration Blueprint

The Nourish Notebook

Transformation Toolkit

Rock Bottom is a Beautiful Place (series of 3 books)

The Art of Brave Living

Dear Female Entrepreneur, My Friend

Information about all of these books and workbooks can be found at **www.DianeCunningham.com/books**, along with links to their Amazon listings. Diane also has a series of magazines and you can flip through them digitally!

inspired ideas *with Diane*

The Inspired Ideas Podcast is an interview-style podcast with host Diane Cunningham Ellis and business owners, entrepreneurs, and guest experts who have successfully created a business they love.

It also includes short tips and trainings on entrepreneurship, mindset, and the Mastermind Effect.

Listen here:
dianecunningham.com/podcast

Or grab it on your favorite podcast directory.

FREE READER RESOURCES

As an exclusive and special gift for readers of this book, I have created a private, reader-only page where you can:

- Download valuable resources, including the Mastermind Checklist, the Questions from this book, bonus trainings and more

- Access links to other videos and trainings on Masterminds

- Get ongoing support by joining my free group where I share daily inspiration and best practices

VISIT

www.DianeCunningham.com/ BookResources

Access your resources now!

Made in the USA
Coppell, TX
16 October 2023

22926549R10077